Wangari's Trees

Written by Nadine Cowan

Illustrated by Nadine Cowan and Katie Crumpton

Collins

CHAPTER 1

Olivia was making her way to Blue Mahoes restaurant when she saw people camping in hammocks up a tree.

Her best friend, Aniyah, and Aniyah's cousin, EJ, were also looking at the tree.

EJ waved. "Hi, Olivia!"

"Mum said that developers want to chop it down and build new flats," explained Aniyah. "Dad said the tree is 150 years old!"

Olivia looked impressed. "So, the tree was growing in Victorian times!"

"*Pfft*, there's no way I'm swapping my comfy bed over one tree," said EJ. "Let's go to Blue Mahoes; I'm hungry!"

"Hungry? You've just had breakfast!" Aniyah replied.

Blue Mahoes was Aniyah and EJ's family restaurant, which served delicious Caribbean food. Inside, billowing steam carried the smell of bay leaves simmering in cornmeal porridge around the restaurant.

"Just in time!" announced Aniyah's dad, as Aniyah, EJ and Olivia stepped through the door. "Cook has just finished frying dumplings! Do you want some?"

Aniyah's dad held out a plate of fried dumplings alongside some sweet plantain.

"EJ, just take one!" said Aniyah's dad.

"Need any help, Uncle?" asked EJ.

"I've got things covered," Aniyah's dad replied.

"Let's go downstairs and play the Ludi game," smiled Olivia.

The Ludi board was Aniyah and EJ's family heirloom. It wasn't just an ordinary board game. It was a magical Ludi board with these words etched on the side:

Roll double six, or double three,

let's learn about your history.

Every time they played, something amazing happened.

First, Aniyah threw a two and a four. Then EJ threw a five and a one. Olivia shook the dice vigorously before releasing them. Double six! Suddenly a puff of iridescent smoke burst from the Ludi board. Blue Mahoes began to fade as a tornado formed a wormhole and pulled them in.

The sky was warm blue and fiery orange, bleeding into pale pink. It was the most beautiful sunrise Aniyah had ever seen.

They were standing on a dirt road in the middle of nowhere. EJ and Aniyah were holding small trees.

"What have you got?" Aniyah asked Olivia.

Olivia inspected the item closely. "I'm not sure. It's some sort of metal tin, with holes on the bottom."

"Look," said Aniyah, nodding to a group of women. They were loading an open-sided truck.

"Who are they? And where are we?" asked EJ.

Before Aniyah could respond, one of the women called out.

"Come on, children. If you could get in the truck before the rainy season that would be great. We have a busy day ahead of us."

"Are you talking to us?" asked EJ.

"Of course," smiled the woman. "I don't see any other children around!"

Aniyah hoisted herself up into the back of the truck. Olivia and EJ followed.

The woman gave them a big, bright smile. "Jambo! I'm Professor Wangari Maathai. Thank you for volunteering. What are your names?"

"I'm Aniyah, this is my cousin EJ, and that's my best friend Olivia."

"Nice to meet you. This is our driver, Amos, and some of our members: Akeyo, Faraja, Hiari, Kioni, Nafula, Zahra and Zuwena." The women nodded as Wangari introduced them.

There were bottles of water, cans, tools and sacks filled with trees in the truck. The trees looked like the ones EJ and Aniyah had. The cans rattled as the truck sped down the road.

"I see you've come prepared," said Wangari.

"Uh, what did we volunteer for exactly?" asked EJ.

Wangari smiled. "To join the Green Belt Movement!"

"What will we do?" asked Olivia, puzzled.

Wangari laughed. "What the Green Belt Movement does best of course ... plant trees!"

"We don't know how to plant trees!" EJ whispered to the others.

Wangari overheard him. "I'll teach you!"

She adjusted her brightly-coloured headwrap. "By the end of today, all these trees will be planted."

Just then, a huge truck came rumbling past on the opposite side of the road. It was carrying wooden logs.

Wangari's smile disappeared. "Loggers! They don't realise how much we depend on the trees."

Akeyo leant over. "It's why we're here."

"That's right," Wangari said. "When I was a little girl, there was a huge fig tree near my home. Beside the tree was a stream, where I played. It felt magical, so magical in fact, my mother warned me that we must never cut down that tree," Wangari's smile reappeared as she remembered.

"In 1964, I left Kenya and travelled to the United States to study. When I returned home, the fig tree was gone!"

"What happened to it?" asked Aniyah.

"It had been chopped down," Wangari replied. "Without the tree, the stream had died, without the water the wildlife had disappeared too – "

She was interrupted by a loud *Bang!* and the truck halted with a thud.

CHAPTER 2

"I think I hit a rock," Amos shouted.

Everyone climbed out of the truck.

"What's that?" Faraja said, pointing at the tyre.

Wangari and Amos looked closely.

"It's a nail," Kioni said.

"The tyre's punctured," said Amos. "But I have a spare."

EJ, Aniyah and Olivia walked back along the road.

"So, we're in Kenya," Olivia said.

"Did you see the newspaper our trees were wrapped in?" EJ replied. "It's 1978!"

"Look!" Aniyah said. "More nails." She picked them up.

"Why would there be nails here?" Olivia asked.

EJ shrugged. "I don't know."

"We're not far from our destination," said Zuwena.

Wangari nodded. "Let's plant these trees while Amos changes the tyre."

Aniyah helped Hiari get a small cart on wheels out of the truck. EJ and Olivia helped the others load it with trees and tools.

Everyone followed Wangari into the forest.

"What happened here?" asked Olivia, as they passed a cluster of tree stumps.

"Deforestation," said Wangari. "All these trees have been cut down. People burn the wood, and the land is used for something else. It's time that changed."

Wangari showed them how to plant a tree.

"This is a Nandi flame tree," she said. "First, dig a large hole like this." Her spade slid into the earth.

EJ held the tree carefully, as Aniyah and Olivia helped to guide it into the hole.

A bird swooped down beside them, grabbed an insect from the disturbed soil, before soaring back up into the sky. Its green and lilac feathers glimmered in the sun.

"Ah, the lilac-breasted roller. Beautiful, isn't it?" smiled Wangari.

"It's not just us that need trees. So many creatures rely on them to survive," explained Wangari. "Without trees, the lilac-breasted roller, and many other animals, would disappear."

They filled the hole around the tree. "Now it needs water," Wangari told them.

Nafula showed Olivia how to fill her tin with water from a large canister.

Olivia's face lit up. "It's a watering can!"

After all the trees had been planted, they returned to the truck.

"Tyre changed, and ready to go," Amos said.

Wangari smiled. "Let's get back to the tree nursery."

They drove down a bumpy road through green pastures. Aniyah looked out of the back of the truck, in awe at the large mountain, silhouetted against the sky.

Amos turned off the road, on to a smaller track.

"What's that smell?" said Aniyah.

Olivia sniffed. "It smells like smoke."

Everyone looked towards the nursery. There was grey smoke rising in the air.

"Fire!" shouted EJ.

CHAPTER 3

Amos slammed on the brakes, and everyone jumped out of the truck.

"Akeyo, Zuwena, grab the hose," Wangari instructed.

There were sparks in the air. Aniyah, Olivia and EJ stomped them out as they reached the ground.

"It was fortunate we arrived when we did," Wangari said.

Olivia looked at the damaged saplings. "I'm glad it was only a small fire, but some of the trees have been destroyed."

"First the nails in the road, and now a fire," Aniyah said.

EJ nodded. "Do you think someone's trying to stop the Green Belt Movement?"

"But why?" Olivia replied.

Wangari overheard them. "Come with me."

She showed them the rest of the tree nursery. There were lots more trees like the ones that got destroyed.

"Streams drying up, poor harvests, no wildlife, lack of firewood … All these things can be improved by planting trees," Wangari told them. "We started with a few trees, and now look!"

"It's amazing," EJ said.

Wangari smiled. "From something small, comes something big. But not everyone agrees with what we're doing. Not everyone sees the long-term benefits."

"Is that why someone left nails in the road?" Olivia asked.

"And started a fire?" Aniyah added.

Wangari sighed. "Honestly? I don't know. What I *do* know is I need your help! We need to clear up and load the truck with more supplies."

"Tea first," said Zuwena, handing them each a cup.

"It's spicy!" Olivia said.

"I've brought some mandazi," Faraja added.

"Faraja makes and sells them at the market," explained Wangari.

EJ shoved one in his mouth. "Mmm ... it's like a doughnut."

"Just take one!" Aniyah said.

"It tastes like my Nanabaa's puff puffs from Ghana," said Olivia.

"There was a time when I was unable to make a living selling them," Faraja told them. "I had no firewood to cook them ... Until Wangari taught me how to plant trees."

"In my village, there was no wood left to build new homes or furniture to put inside them," explained Akeyo. "Until Wangari encouraged us to plant more trees to replace the ones we were chopping down."

"Every one of these women's lives have been impacted by deforestation in some way," said Wangari.

"Yes," nodded Nafula. "People were starving, and the streams had all dried up. We were desperate for water to drink and to water our crops. Wangari advised us to plant more trees."

Suddenly, there was an almighty *Crash!* Everyone jumped.

CHAPTER 4

They ran outside to find one of the nursery gates wide open. Goats had got in and were eating the trees!

"I thought I closed the gates," said Wangari, confused.

"You did," Olivia replied. "*Someone* must have opened them!"

Aniyah caught sight of two boys. "I bet it was them," she said.

The boys made a run for it, but Aniyah and EJ
were quicker.

"We're sorry!" one of the boys cried. "We wanted to see
the tree lady and the goats got in."

"Did you start a fire earlier?" EJ asked.

"And throw nails in the road?" Aniyah added.

The boys shook their heads. "We don't know anything
about that."

"Well, you can explain yourselves to 'the tree lady',"
Aniyah replied.

Wangari gave the boys a hard stare. "You can clear up the mess," she told them. "*And* load the van."

She turned to Aniyah, EJ and Olivia. "Thank you for solving that mystery."

"Maybe you can figure out which one of my children have been sneaking into the pan and helping themselves to my mandazi!" smiled Faraja.

"Easy! Check for sticky fingers!" Aniyah laughed.

"Amos says the fire may have been caused by the sun on dried leaves," Wangari told them.

"What about the nails?" Olivia asked.

"I'm not sure we'll ever know if that was deliberate or not. But they'll be useful to mend the gate!" Wangari smiled.

Suddenly, a colourful cloud appeared. "Time to go," Aniyah said.

"Well, at least they've got two more 'volunteers'," EJ replied.

The sunset faded, a tornado that formed a wormhole pulled them in and they arrived back at Blue Mahoes. They could hear Cook singing in the kitchen.

"I'm going to ask my parents if we can plant more trees in our garden," said Aniyah.

"Good idea," said EJ. "I wish there was something we could do to help the people protesting. Saving the tree is the right thing to do."

"Wangari said something small can make a big difference," Aniyah replied.

Olivia nodded. "I have an idea. We'll need some card and marker pens."

PLANT A TREE!

1. Get organised.

2. Dig a big hole.

3. Plant a tree.

4. Water and mulch.

5. Grow some more trees.

6. Save old trees.

REAL PEOPLE

Wangari Maathai 1940-2011

Professor Wangari Maathai was the first African woman to win a Nobel Peace Prize. As part of the Green Belt Movement, Wangari mobilised thousands of people to plant trees in Kenya. She spent her life campaigning for action to be taken to combat climate change; the Green Belt Movement has planted more than 50 million trees.

Ideas for reading

Written by Gill Matthews
Primary Literacy Consultant

Reading objectives:
- check that the book makes sense to them, discussing their understanding and exploring the meaning of words in context
- predict what might happen from details stated and implied
- summarise the main ideas drawn from more than one paragraph, identifying key details that support the main ideas

Spoken language objectives:
- ask relevant questions to extend their understanding and knowledge
- use relevant strategies to build their vocabulary
- articulate and justify answers, arguments and opinions
- participate in discussions, presentations, performances, role play, improvisations and debates

Curriculum links: Geography – Human and physical geography

Interest words: mobilised, campaigning, action, combat

Build a context for reading
- Ask children to look closely at the front cover and to read the title.
- Read the back-cover blurb.
- Ask children what they think might happen in the story.

Understand and apply reading strategies
- Read pp2–5 aloud, using meaning, dialogue and punctuation to help you to read with appropriate expression.
- Ask children what they have learnt about EJ, Olivia and Aniyah so far.
- Ask children to read pp6–12 quietly to themselves using the techniques you demonstrated earlier to help them read with expression.
- Ask children to summarise what has happened so far in the story.
- Discuss what they think might happen next. Encourage them to support their predictions with reasons and evidence from the text.
- Give children the opportunity to read the rest of the book, pausing to summarise what happens in each chapter and to predict what might happen next.